HABITS FOR LEADERS GROUNDED & GROWING

AARON MARSHALL, PHD

For those who long for deeper roots & greater harvests.

WHAT READERS ARE SAYING

The content is great, but the delivery is what really shines - metaphors, personal examples, and practical steps forward.

VICTOR

Great insights. The tips are relevant and useful in everyday life - especially for time management and networking.

SOODEH

I REALLY enjoyed this learning. I took copious notes & plan on picking up a couple of the books you reference. Thank you, and really well done!

KELLIE

Beautiful sharing on how to live a life of peace and strength.

DOUG

The habit of building quiet in my life really resonated with me - especially as my level of responsibility (at work) increases. Great content!

PAUL

This hooked me in the first few minutes!

ROBIN

This is full of excellent tips which any executive can use in their daily activities over the long term.

B.K.

Amazing Content! Thank you Aaron.

LADAN

I'm inspired by the message to reframe goals, but what resonated most was learning to "assume positive intent." Thank you!

DAVE

Every good that is worth possessing must be paid for in strokes of daily effort.

WILLIAM JAMES

CONTENTS

INTRODUCTION

> *My friends say I shouldn't compare everything to Bruce Willis movies, but you know what they say about old habits... they Pulp Fiction.*

People have written thousands of books on how to be a great leader. From high level strategy to thoughtful research into company culture, to entire workshops devoted to the best models of executive leadership.

But, what about the minutia of leadership development?

What makes a successful leader day in and day out? How do you - as a leader - balance everything on your shoulders and still stay sane? How do you achieve - as the ancient philosophers asked - the good life, while leading your team or organization to success?

That's what I want to offer you in this brief book - twenty manageable and beneficial habits you can build into your life to get you one step closer to flourishing as a leader.

Just to be clear, I'm no habits guru. I've learned from others how to build meaningful practices into my life. I can tell you that these practices have significant benefits.

I first got excited about *intentional habit formation* while studying Aristotle in grad school. As you'll see in what follows, I lean on my studies (Philosophy MA, Education PhD, and MBA) and professional experience (C-suite executive, NPO founder, and leadership coach) to share what has worked for me. I'll also sneak in research occasionally to support why these habits actually do transform lives.

Bottom line - experience continues to teach me what works and what doesn't - as I live a life with multiple responsibilities.

I'm sure you can relate.

In this book, I'll give you habits to keep you grounded and habits to help you stay disciplined; habits for handling your relationships, and habits to help you become a more discerning thinker.

Are you ready to consider some new ways of being in the world? If so, let's get started.

HOW TO USE THIS BOOK

Before diving into the habits, the first section "Why Habits?" talks about what habits are and how they work. These chapters may feel less practical, as they lay a foundation for how to think about habits.

The rest of the book is broken into four categories:

- Habits for the Grounded Self
- Habits for the Disciplined Self
- Habits for the Relational Self
- Habits for the Discerning Self

In some ways, the order builds - so there will be some advantage to reading from start to finish. That said, each chapter can stand alone.

If you're itching to jump ahead and need permission - you've got it.

Each habit chapter shares some context, followed by practical tips for starting that habit. The subheading "Ready. Set. Go." is your reminder to use this book practically. That heading shows up right before I lay out simple steps for establishing the new habit.

I wrote this as a *practical tool* to help you get results. As you start developing habits, remember not to try them all at once. Instead, pace yourself.

Set manageable goals so you can stick with each habit you want to cultivate.

You bought the book - that means you have access to these habits forever. Don't feel like you need to take on each practice the day you read it. I recommend picking one or two at a time. Spend a few months making those habits consistent parts of your life. Reflect on the value of the habits.

When those habits become automatic, add another. When possible, look for opportunities to stack them (*stacking* is like fertilizer for a habit).

ADDITIONAL RESOURCES

Finally, forming new habits can be tough - especially on your own, with a book. Reading is only step one.

We've developed many additional resources to support you on your "grounded & growing" leadership journey:

- *Get Connected* by joining the Facebook group, connecting/following me on LinkedIn, joining a Habits for Leaders cohort, or attending a Grounded & Growing experience.
- Download our *"Ready. Set. Go. Worksheets"* so you can do the reflective work after each chapter.
- Download bonus *"Grounding Exercises"* to clarify who you are and what you are about in this life.
- Track Your Growth using our *Individual Commitment Worksheet* and *Habit Tracker*.

All these resources are available at

https://habitsforleadersbooklaunch.carrd.co

I look forward to seeing you there.
In the meantime, enjoy the book!

PART ONE
WHY HABITS?

CHAPTER 1
YOUR HABIT

TIME FOR A NEW OUTFIT

> *I turned down a laundry job at the monastery.*
> *I didn't want to pick up dirty habits.*

MONASTIC ORDERS FASCINATE ME. Each has an aim, specific vows, a rule or way of life, and a community. Benedictine monks, for instance, vow obedience (listening to God), stability (lifelong submission to the Rule and to an Abbott), and fidelity (which includes poverty and chastity).

Their vow plays out daily through routines, practices, and rhythms that shape and reshape the Benedictine monk's character.

In addition to the vow, Benedictine monks wear a black *cowl* – a full cloak with wide sleeves and a hood. Do you know what that plain yet distinctive outfit, worn day in and day out, is called? If you guessed "a *habit*," collect two gold stars.

You and I are a lot like the Benedictine monk.

We wear our own *habits*. Like the black cowl, our own habits shape our behavior and our identity.

> None of us are *habit-less*. We are, as they say, creatures of habit.

Following the analogy, your bad habits are simply the wrong clothes. I'm guessing you picked up this book in search of new habits - or at least the success new habits can offer.

First, you'll need to take a look at the old habits. What's working for you? What's not?

For those that don't work, strip them away. Don't throw them in the wash. Throw them out. It's time to go shopping for new cowl - a new set of practices.

Not only are you already wearing habits - the good and the bad - you've already submitted yourself to a *rule of life*. You just might not realize it. You probably didn't list out your current habits and commit to them, but your life is already defined by your routines and practices. These patterns form an implicit *rule of life* - parallel to the Benedictine monk's explicit vows. It turns out actions *do* speak louder than words.

YOU CAN CHANGE YOUR HABIT.

Here's the good news: if you want to change, you can. You can try on new clothes. You can sign on to a new *rule of life*.

In what follows, you'll learn about 20 habits - twenty pieces of clothing you can choose to put on. As you do, reflect on the habits you already wear, and the *rule of life* it communicates to you and those around you.

Remember, life doesn't just happen to you. You make choices everyday.

Take a good, hard look in the mirror. You get to choose which routines, practices, and rhythms serve you well, and which do not. Which you will put on, and which you will strip away.

Monastic orders expanded because people longed to live more *intentionally* – do you?

Early Benedictines sought peace and simplicity. Early Jesuits sought education and social justice. Centuries later, those core commitments still identify members of those monastic communities. That kind of reputation lasts because individuals continue to take up daily routines and practices that cultivate value-driven lives of virtue.

   Do you want to live intentionally?

It may seem counter-intuitive, but monks experience freedom when they submit to a rule of life.

Did you catch that? Submitting to a *rule of life* provides the grounding and structure necessary for real freedom and flourishing - purpose and direction.

The same is true for me, and it can be true for you too. Submitting to the discipline of new practices, rearranging your routines, and establishing rhythms *will* crimp your autonomy.

It will also clarify your purpose and give you direction, unlocking unexpected freedom along the way. Are you willing to submit - to endure some short term pain for the sake of a bigger and better horizon?

READY. SET. GO.

Before turning the page, take a moment to reflect.

- What about your current habit serves you well?
- What about your current habit needs to change?
- What are you willing to give up in order to achieve the life you want?

CHAPTER 2
HABIT FERTILIZER
HUMAN FLOURISHING IS POSSIBLE

> *What do you call a fruit that's rough around the edges?*
>
> *A bad apple.*

EVER WONDER how trees grow fruit?

Picture an apple tree with a large canopy of branches and a robust trunk planted solidly in rich soil. Imagine the surrounding landscape shifting rapidly through seasons in a time-lapse sequence - leaves coloring, then falling as temperatures drop, then snowfall, then the steady melt and buzz of spring along with new leaves and fresh buds.

On the outside, the tree withstands the elements.

What's happening inside that tree as the seasons pass? What prepares that tree to produce apples?

When teaching ethics, I ask students to picture themselves as that tree, mustering the will power necessary to grow an apple. Squinting their eyes, focusing their attention, and forcing a few grunts. Looking to their fingertips for the first signs of red fruit.

Perhaps, with enough effort, an apple will form in their outstretched hands.

Perhaps not. Sheer willpower does not grow apples.

> Ironically, we try to produce "fruit" in our own lives exactly the same way.

We squint our eyes, focus our energy, and will ourselves toward healthier diets and more efficient work sessions. And, when our will power fades - and it always does - our outstretched hand remains empty.

A RELIABLE PATTERN

On real apple trees, fresh fruit "appears" reliably, year after year – at the appropriate time, in the appropriate way. And the tree doesn't waste energy feeling anxious about it.

Apples develop on tree branches after months of healthy roots planted in the right kind of soil. After seasons of adequate sunlight and water. After the timely cross-pollination of flowers.

Cultivating habits depends on similar conditions. When's the last time you checked your soil, sunlight, and water?

Habits researcher and USC Provost Professor of Psychology and Business, Wendy Wood, calls out context, repetition, and reward as the essential conditions necessary for successful habit formation.

Context drives your ability to form habits. The world is full of forces that add or reduce friction to cultivating new habits. It's a lot easier to form habits when friction is low.

Repetition establishes your new habit. It'd be great if a habit always formed after sixty days of practice. Unfortunately, there's no magic number of times you need to do something before it becomes a habit.

Habits kick in silently, in ways you won't notice until well after the practice is automatic. Until then, you'll have to consistently choose the new behavior.

There are ways to make choosing a habit easier. Wood suggests stacking habits (discussed more in chapter 11), swapping habits, cueing up the behaviors you want, and making quicker decisions when the context is set. All these suggestions ease friction and make habit formation a bit easier.

> "With regular intention, we stop consulting our intentions and just keep acting."
>
> WENDY WOOD

In other words, what starts as practiced behavior eventually becomes muscle memory. What starts as a stack - placing nighttime medication on a bedside table with a water bottle - soon fades to the background, automated within the context of bedtime routine. What starts as a swap - drinking bubbly water instead of a beer during the week - soon fades to the background, automated by the familiar cold aluminum can and CO_2.

When you cue up new behaviors and repeatedly, consistently practice them, muscle memory develops and the behavior triggers without conscious decision-making.

Context and repetition are important, but without *reward*, your new habit won't stick.

What rewards work best? Use ice cream sparingly. Intrinsic rewards are stronger than extrinsic. Also, avoiding guilt and obligation isn't much of a reward - they are both poor motivators.

Instead of guilting yourself into a workout, reframe exercise. Do you exercise as a way to energize your day? To get time with a friend? When reframing, consider how the new habit connects with your bigger goals in life.

Aristotle argues that everything we do aims at something that aims at something that aims at something, until it aims at the ultimate aim - *human flourishing*.

> "Every craft and every line of inquiry, and likewise every action and decision, seems to seek some good; that is why some people were right to describe *the good* as that which everyone seeks."
>
> ARISTOTLE

Back to exercise - I don't workout for pleasure, though I might enjoy it from time to time. Guilt is a poor motivator, and avoiding guilt isn't much of a reward. So, I reframe exercise. I don't work out because I have to, or even because exercise is good. I work out because I value my health. And, I value health because I think it contributes to my overall happiness, or flourishing.

American Philosopher and longtime USC professor Dallas Willard identifies a similar "reliable pattern" for lasting character formation: vision, intention, and means.

Following Willard, habits stick when you've clearly *imagined* how things could be, *chosen and committed* to pursue that end, and when you've taken up the appropriate *tools* to accomplish the task.

Pulling together the frameworks offered by Willard and Wood, let's recap.

Starting a new habit requires more than effort and willpower. Consider the *context* of your habit action. Can you arrange things to make habit execution easier? Consider the frequency of *repetition*. Are there cues you can plant in advance to encourage repeating the practice? Perhaps you can stack the new habit directly after an established habit, or create visual cues to remind yourself of the habit and why you want to establish it. Consider the power of *reward*. What intrinsic benefits will the new habit provide? Finally, how does the new habit fit into your personal values and *vision*?

These concepts - context, repetition, reward, vision, intention, means - help as we cultivate specific habits. They're the fertilizer that feeds our habits. Get these right, and you'll escape the "Nike" approach to habit formation. No one can "just do it." Even the best of us fail to muster the necessary willpower. But despair not. Habits become automatic, like muscle memory.

> A habit turns the world around you into a trigger to act. The situation you're in triggers the response from memory, and you act. It can essentially bypass your executive mind. The pleasure is in the thing getting done without you consciously lifting a finger.
>
> WENDY WOOD

The bulk of this book (chapters 4-23) introduce specific habits worth forming. Each habit represents a *means* that supports our attempts to thrive - to live flourishing lives.

Before exploring those specific *means* to flourish, the next chapter takes a deeper look at Willard's reliable pattern.

Are you ready to establish your vision and set your intention? These are your first steps toward growing new fruit.

READY. SET. GO.

Before turning the page, take a moment to reflect.

- What examples of context, repetition, and reward do you see in your current routines?
- Describe your vision for your life in an elevator pitch. Now in a eulogy.

CHAPTER 3
VISION & INTENTION
SET A COURSE AND BURN
THE SHIPS

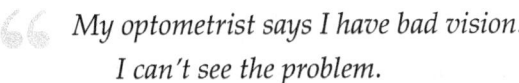 *My optometrist says I have bad vision.*
I can't see the problem.

LASTING personal and social development begins with a vision. Many of my coaching clients struggle with identifying their *vision* – and for a variety of reasons.

Do any of these sound like you?

- You don't want to settle on one vision for the future because it will exclude others.
- You don't want to get too clear about where you're going because you might not get there and that would be a disappointing failure.
- You're more of a go with the flow kind of person, and imaging the future feels rigid and boxy. Isn't it the journey that matters most?

- You like to get things done, but vision sounds fuzzy and soft – ain't nobody got time for that.
- Insert your own reason here.

Each concern carries *some* truth:

- Choosing a particular vision *does* eliminate others.
- Clarity *does* carry the weight of potential failure.
- Casting a vision *does* require planning and structure.
- Vision is a fuzzy, future-thinking exercise lacking certainty.

Ouch. So, why waste time developing a clear vision?

Well, as the pinstripe philosopher Yogi Berra once said,

> "If you don't know where you're going, you'll end up someplace else."

The truth is, you're already on your way. But where are you going? Is your vision directed by long term hopes and dreams or are you like most people - too distracted by the urgency of today to pause and ask for directions?

START BY DREAMING

It's time to pause. Time to clear your head and dream a little. As you cast a vision for your life, think broadly. Include vocation, location, and family – but don't stop there.

Go further. Way further.

Think about the big stuff – deep hopes and longings. Think about the kind of person you want to become. Think about your strengths and passions. Imagine how those unique talents could impact your family, friends, and community.

You'll know you're closing in on real "visiony" stuff when you start getting excited about chasing that horizon – when you'd give up whatever it takes to become that kind of person.[1]

Remember that habit you're wearing? You might need new clothes to chase down your new horizon.

COMMIT TO CHANGE

Remember that rule of life? Habits take effort and discipline. Are you willing to set aside short term desires for the sake of your bigger vision?

If so, it's time to settle your *intention*.

Intention is about making a clear decision and sticking to it. Choosing the compelling vision that stirs up your insides and letting go of fears and anxieties holding you captive. Intention requires you to announce your own set of vows - for your monastic order of one.

Intention moves you past *wanting* or *wishing*. It is a *declared* commitment.

Are you ready for that?

If you're not yet sure about your vision for life, that's okay. Habits 1 & 2 will help you find clarity. At this point, commit yourself to change. Commit to doing the hard work of finding a vision that drives you. Set that intention, and use this book as a tool to chase that horizon.

READY. SET. GO.

Before turning the page, take a moment to reflect.

- Review the bulleted list at the top of the chapter. Which bullets most resonate with you? Why?
- Make a list of the fears and anxieties holding you back. Read over your list and interrogate your fears. Are there false beliefs hiding behind them? Surface those false beliefs and interrogate them.

PART TWO
HABITS FOR THE GROUNDED SELF

Being grounded is the key to being fruitful.

DR. PREM JAGYASI

CHAPTER 4
HABIT 1
KNOW WHO | IDENTITY

> *Shout out to all my friends going through an identity crisis. You know who you are... I think.*

SUCCESSFUL EXECUTIVES HAVE this mysterious quality dubbed "executive presence" – a sort of engaged confidence that comes from a clear sense of self, voice, position, and opportunity. At its core, executive presence is about *grounded-ness*.

To develop this "executive presence," you'll need to be honest about who you are today. You'll have to get comfortable in your own skin.

You'll also need to get clear about *who* you are becoming. Not what you will achieve, or who you will spend time with, but the *kind of person* you are becoming.

This notion of *becoming* has a long and rich history. Aristotle, for instance, argued that just as an acorn aims to become a mighty oak, you aim to become a certain kind of person.

Intentionally or not, the habits and routines that make up your life shape who you are becoming.

This is really good news.

Life doesn't just happen to you. If your current habits and routines aren't helping you get where you need to go, you can change them.

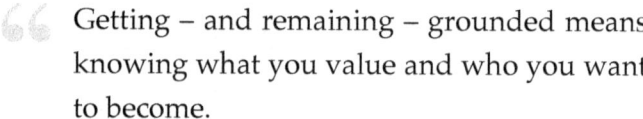 Getting – and remaining – grounded means knowing what you value and who you want to become.

READY. SET. GO.

Here's an easy exercise to get you started and a habit to keep you grounded.

First, draft a simple personal statement that captures your values in an aspirational way. Who do you want to become – what will be absolutely true about future you?

This personal statement will be a lens – a way to gut check all your other habits and routines to make sure they support you becoming the kind of person you really want to be.

So, keep it simple.

Create a mind map that identifies your values, strengths, and passions – all the combinations of quali-ties that already make you, uniquely you. Then, add in the qualities you most want to be true of future you – characteristics you aim for but have not yet fully real-ized. These are the qualities you still need to "live into."

I like to use a whiteboard, but a piece of paper will

work fine. Let it be messy. I like to start with values, so I might write "being on mission with people" in the center. What's a driving value for you? Write it in the center. Then, draw a few lines out from that comment. Start adding values, strengths, passions, or examples, and build from there. The goal is to write a lot in a short period of time. There's no need to judge your ideas or prioritize at this stage - just get your thoughts down.

Next, turn your mind map into a simple sentence – using three adjectives and a noun:

I am a (adjective), (adjective), (adjective), (noun)!

For example, I've had clients say things like:

- I am a powerful, resourceful, compassionate leader.
- I am a courageous, empathetic, wise advocate.
- I am an inclusive, partnership-building, problem-solving pioneer

If you don't love your first version, tweak it. Once you have it right, commit to reading it, out loud, daily. Let your personal statement empower you to live with intention.

If you do, *future you* will thank you.

CHAPTER 5
HABIT 2
KNOW WHY | PURPOSE

66 *What do you call a knife with no purpose?*
Pointless.

WHAT QUESTION DO you find so compelling that you will spend your life chasing an answer? I got to ask a number of undergrads this question while teaching their social entrepreneurship class. For those early twenty-somethings, honing in on a clear answer proved difficult. It's one thing to choose a major. It's another entirely to identify that passion we most want to pursue.

As an enneagram 7[1], I still struggle with this question. I spend my life chasing lots of valuable pursuits that bring me joy. If it were up to me, I'd do everything. Unfortunately, as mid-life approaches (or flies by) I am increasingly faced with the prospect that *doing everything* may not be realistic (or possible) in this life.

Looking back on my life with closer to 20/20 hindsight, I can trace some threads through my own circuitous journey. Deep values like *be on mission with a team, stay curious*, and *coach others up* weave my otherwise disparate experiences into a beautiful tapestry. Rather than a happy accident, it's because I've spent years listening and attending to how these values play out that my disconnected *doing everything* has a deeply connected *why*.

Have you learned to articulate the gut drive that compels you to do what you do? Successful leaders work at getting clear about their deepest passions and how those passions might play out in the world. They think about their "why." Simon Sinek suggests *starting with why*.

> "People don't buy what you do, they buy why you do it."
>
> SIMON SINEK

I think he's right, and when you look in the mirror – when you turn the believing and doing inward, you start to see that you aren't driven by some rational plan.

> You are driven by a desire, a love, a calling, a purpose.

Successful executives are crystal clear about why they do what they do. They understand their calling - their purpose.

Do you? Can you articulate it?

READY. SET. GO.

I've got a quick exercise that will help you get clear about your purpose – your why. Then a practice so that you can train yourself to act intentionally, in line with your purpose.

It's not a complicated practice, but it requires consistency. To work, it must become a habit.

First, you'll need to get crystal clear about your "why."

Now, there's more than one way to wash this window. I'll offer two. Either approach can be done in 30-40 minutes.

Option 1 – start writing down questions you find compelling, questions you could spend a lifetime chasing. Write freely for a few minutes, then review the 5-10 questions in front of you. What do they have in common? What themes emerged? Now, use those themes to draft new questions – questions that get closer to capturing that bigger sense of calling and purpose.

Or, try Option 2 – Imagine future you, at some specific age 20, 30, or even 40 years down the road. Brainstorm a list of all the things you hope will be true of future you. Think about your work, your health, your relationships, your hobbies, and your finances.

Write freely for a few minutes, then start interrogating your list. For each item, simply ask yourself "why?" State your answer out loud. Then ask "why" of your answer. Repeat this process a few times for each item on your list. As you work through your list, and your answers, listen for themes.

Once you've completed either option 1 or option 2, try to articulate your why – your calling or purpose - in a succinct way.

It'll sound something like, "I want _____ so that _____ because _____."

Now for the hard part – consistency. To live intentionally, to grow in your calling or purpose, you'll need to keep it front of mind. Write it down.

Place it somewhere you'll see it consistently – a bathroom mirror, a bedside table, your computer monitor – and when you see it, read it aloud.

Do this consistently, and your "why" will influence your other routines and practices. As Simon Sinek says later in his talk, "what you do just proves what you believe." When you begin to live out your purpose, your actions follow.

CHAPTER 6

HABIT 3
PRACTICE QUIET

> *Did you see the advert for a really quiet guitar?*
> *No strings attached.*

I ATTENDED my first real concert as a first year undergrad in Northwest Oregon. A group of us piled into a tiny yellow Volkswagen Rabbit and headed to a small club in Southeast Portland where a Ska band from Couer d'lena Idaho was setting up. Trombones, drums, and electric guitar reverberated through the small club as several hundred of us pressed toward the stage in a classic 90s mosh pit. When the concert ended I was soaked in sweat, smelled like smoke, and my ears hummed from the amplification. I couldn't hear myself think. We piled into the Rabbit and headed back to campus reliving the show. It was epic.

Now, that hum in my ear feels like every day. Did you know that your life is louder and more distracting than over ninety percent of all humans who have ever lived – and the noise in our lives just keeps getting louder.

Just as electric lights change the way we see stars in cities, that constant hum in our ears changes how we hear hear ourselves and others. In leadership, this constant noice causes problems. Noise will escalate stress and feelings of urgency. It will limit your ability to attend to your own thoughts and feeling - much less the thoughts and feelings of those you lead.

For these reasons, successful leaders practice quiet – quieting your physical environment, and quieting the highway of distractions racing through your mind.

This whole notion of quiet draws on ancient disciplines of solitude, silence, and stillness. While similar, each taps into a distinct aspect of quieting oneself.

Solitude, invites you to be alone. I've heard from many introverted friends - especially through the pandemic - that solitude has been a welcome relief. As an extreme extrovert, I struggle to spend time alone. Yet, I have experienced the value of alone time, especially as it prepares me to be more present when I have the opportunity to be with others.

Silence invites external quiet. As a verbal processor and extrovert, I spend a lot of time talking. It helps me clarify my thinking and the thinking of those around me. It helps me build relationships. It allows me to participate in music as I belt out tunes in the shower and on my commute. None of those are bad things. Yet, the practice of silence regulates my verbal output. It invites me to create airtime for others, for the musician, for running water, or wind rustling leaves. As a practice, silence will quiet your input by quieting your voice.

Stillness invites internal quiet. When I carve time for reflective practice, my mind races with to-dos, upcoming conversations, problems that need to be solved - stillness invites me to set those distractions aside and listen. In stillness, I wait. I work to set aside the pending pressures and mental distractions in favor of quiet.

These practices show up across the ancient world, and neuroscience confirms this ancient wisdom.

When used as a control in a study testing the effect of different kinds of music, silence outperformed even relaxation music as the most beneficial. Silence allows your brain to process in a default state.[1]

In another study, two hours of daily silence led to cell development in the hippocampus, strengthening memory formation.[2]

> Practicing quiet won't just re-energize you,
> it will literally grow your brain.

What would it look like to carve space each day for quiet?

I've got a few ideas for you.

READY. SET. GO.

First, consider your work schedule. You probably already have a productivity rhythm – a natural pace of engaged work followed by disengaged rest. Unfortunately, you likely also disengage with a screen – whether that's binging Netflix or scrolling on your phone.

Swap some of that disengaged rest for real brain rest - preferably with quiet.

Create a rhythm of work and rest so your brain receives small power naps throughout the day. Schedule these times – even if they are solo walks that last just 5 minutes.

Second, imagine carving time for a longer period of quiet once a day. Could you start work a bit later? Could you wake up a bit earlier? Could you extend your lunch break?

Carving time literally suggests whittling away less important things. What will you say "No" to or eliminate so that quiet can become a priority?

Identify a time that works for you, and begin. Being quiet actually takes practice. I recommend you combine all three ancient disciplines to start – solitude, silence, and stillness. Find an alone space far from the bustle of normal life, and quiet yourself inside and out.

Beware, when you take up this practice your mind will fight you. That's okay - you'll be ready. Settle in with a pen and journal. As your mind races, simply jot down the thoughts that you can't easily dismiss. Then, return to quiet.

Take pressure off your brain by attending to your other senses. Pay attention to your breathing. The important part is letting distraction fade into the background. Resist the urge to pick up your phone. Just be quiet.

In the beginning, just a few minutes will feel painful. Consistent practice will change that, so be gracious with yourself.

WARNING

Early on, this practice will feel like a waste of time. Be patient. Lean in. In time, you will experience the strength and grounded-ness that flows out of practicing quiet.

CHAPTER 7
HABIT 4
DRAW STRENGTH

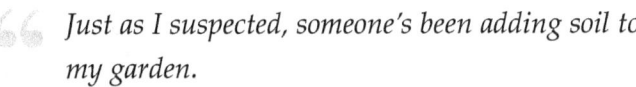 *Just as I suspected, someone's been adding soil to my garden.*
The plot thickens.

I HAVE an orange tree in my front drive. Given the appropriate temperature, sunlight, and water, that tree provides our family with baskets full of citrus delight each winter. My kids love to collect and juice them – there's nothing quite like a glass of fresh squeezed orange juice.

That little tree draws its strength from several tap roots, or anchor roots, and a web of shallower roots reaching out from the trunk. These roots pull water and nutrients up into the tree, promoting health. All this strength supports the tree in growing fruit.

You too need strength. Leadership fruit, or success, requires habits that draw strength like the roots of my orange tree. You'll need to develop habits – rhythms of life – that grow a few deep tap roots, and spread many shallower ones. I realize this sounds a little "chicken and egg" - do you draw strength to develop habits or do the habits draw strength for you? In reality it's a bit of both.

Part of drawing strength comes from your understanding of personal identity and purpose. Your *lens for living* - what you believe to be true about yourself and this world - establishes a context for identifying soil. My soil is a mix of family norms, and my faith foundation which informs how I make sense of those existential questions like "Who am I?" and "Why am I here?"

My faith grounds me – like an anchor root – so that even if strong winds strip away my leaves, I remain rooted in that existential understanding. I am anchored by my beliefs, and their associated promises and hopes. This phenomenon is not just religious. We all have answers to those questions - whether or not we have articulated them explicitly. We all have a *lens for living*. Often, the greatest pull against our rootedness comes from the storms in life that challenge that lens. These storms highlight perceived and felt conflicts between your beliefs about reality and your lived experience.

On the other side, habits like the quiet (unpacked in chapter 6) create regular reflective space for you to make your *lens for living* more front of mind and wrestle through points of incoherence. In this way, regular rhythms of reflective practice help roots grow in breadth and depth.

So, how do you create a habit of drawing strength?

READY. SET. GO.

First, reflect on the soil you are planted in. Socrates' quip to "know thyself" is a powerful reminder from the ancient world that humanity has always been distracted. For many, it is easier to take the busy-ness of each day as it comes. Existential questions don't get lunches packed or projects wrapped. But the big questions do matter. They inform identity and purpose. They root us for coming storms. So, work on making your *lens for living* a bit more explicit. Follow the ancient wisdom and get more comfortable in your own skin. As you increasingly know yourself, you'll increasingly be able to better lead yourself, and in turn lead others.

As you become clear about soil that grounds you, pay attention to the reflective practices that helped you grow those *strength drawing* roots. For me, this looks like carving time each day to read and pray within my faith context. This is a chance for me to push deeper roots into the soil – to ask hard questions and release things outside my control. Like the orange tree tugging up nutrients, this time feeds my soul.

You might grow roots by walking in a forest or along the beach, realigning your lived experience with deeper beliefs about reality. You might carve time for meditation. You might find a liturgy or mantra to repeat that energizes you. All these rhythms support drawing strength from your soil.

As you get started, take heed. Like many habits, growing roots can feel painfully slow. Especially in easier seasons of life, these rhythms can feel unproductive and inefficient. But when the proverbial storms come, you'll want established roots to hold you in place, grounding you.

Whatever practices you choose to establish, make sure they grow your roots into the soil you want anchoring you. Then, lean on those practices to pull nutrients up – drawing the strength you need to remain grounded.

CHAPTER 8
HABIT 5
CULTIVATE COURAGE

> *Which has more courage, a rock or a tree?*
> *A rock - it's boulder!*

A HEADLINE earlier this year read, "60 percent of U.S. adults are feeling daily stress and worry." Nearly one in five adults experience diagnosable anxiety.

If executive success depends on remaining grounded, watch out for stress, worry, and anxiety. These fire breathing dragons pose an existential challenge to your executive knighthood, and the key to being knighted is cultivating courage.[1]

Aristotle describes courage as the virtue between two vices – cowardice and rashness. According to the philosopher, courageous action depends on your ability to mediate your fear appropriately, and act in light of it.

Let me explain. Imagine you are a hero/heroine in a medieval village, and a messenger of the king has just announced that a nearby dragon is villainously terrorizing neighboring villages. This is your quest for the taking. *Set aside the ethics of dragon slaying, and go with me here.*

How do you respond, and what does it have to do with courage?

If you are a coward, you might board up your home inside the Kingdom, and call it a day. Cowardice is a vice of courage.

If you're rash, you might race out of the city in your skivvies with only a frying pan to swing at the dragon. Rashness is the other vice of courage.

> Both vices misread the situation, allowing fear to either grow (cowardice) or shrink (rashness) out of its appropriate proportion.

You, however, are not rash or a coward. You are brave.

As the courageous hero/heroine, you are still afraid, but you recognize that duty calls, and keeping fear at its proper measure, you put on the right armor and take up the right tools to complete your quest.

Acting courageously is double hard to cultivate because as we practice, we tend toward vice. That means practicing courage should feel uncomfortable. For example, if you currently tend toward more cowardly behavior, practicing a brave act will *feel* rash to you. On the other hand, if you tend toward more rash behavior, practicing a brave act will *feel* cowardly. Aristotle likens this process to bending a curved stick back to straight - it must be bent past straight for a time, so that in the end it settles straight.

The point is this: courageous action will be uncomfortable. That's exactly why you need to practice being brave.

READY. SET. GO.

So, what are the proverbial dragons leaders must slay? Start with stress, worry, and anxiety. I've got a few simple habits to share that will help you cultivate courage.

First, pay attention to your social media use. The rise of anxiety in America parallels our accelerating use of social media platforms. These platforms promote comparison, present unachievable goals, invite unhealthy judgement, and rewire our brains like chemical addiction.

Pay attention, limit your use, or dump it completely. This will take daily courage – resisting the urge to participate. Practice self-control.

Next, take inventory of your stress and worries. In his book on executive success, Scott Elbin explains that as leaders advance in their careers, they must learn to "pick up accountability for many results" while letting go of "responsibility for a few results."

This shift to high level, broad accountability can come without the felt sense of control many leaders are used to maintaining. Accountability without a clear sense of control can quickly feel like stress and worry. The trouble is, at higher levels of an organization, you simply can't quality check everything that flows through your divisions. You've got to step back and build the team you can trust, coach them up, and get out of the way.

Stress and worry are strongest when you lack power and face uncertainty. The felt lack of control grows when you trade in self-reliance for team reliance. Most often, courage will invite you to pause and acknowledge what is - and is not - within your control.

Don't give in to stress by abdicating your position or doubling down to force your way. Those approaches reflect the vicious knights – one boarded up at home, and the other charred in front the dragon's lair.

Instead, practice courage by allowing stress its appropriate measure – a helpful indicator that something is out of balance, and a reminder to take stock of what is yours to control and yours to let go.

How ever you cultivate courage, you can be sure of this, the more you practice, the better prepared you will be to face the dragon when the quest is offered.

PART THREE
HABITS FOR THE
DISCIPLINED SELF

Discipline is choosing between what you want now, and what you want most.

ABRAHAM LINCOLN

CHAPTER 9
HABIT 6
PRACTICE EARLY WINS

> *I posted a joke about inertia earlier, but it doesn't seem to be gaining any momentum.*

IF YOU WANT to conquer the world, you need some early wins.

The original Nintendo came out when I was nine, and several of my relatives conspired against my parents to surprise my brother and I with one for Christmas. Many childhood hours were spent conquering some world – level by level.

Occasionally, my brother and I would deem a game too easy or too hard, but most games had an uncanny ability to suck us in and hold our attention. I remember one night in particular that I spent at neighbor's house. We rented a game and started in on level one around dinner time. About lunchtime the next morning, we finished.

What kept us going? Other than the inane pleasure staying awake can be for an elementary kid, we stuck with it because we believed we could beat the game. And, we believed we could beat the game because we were able to beat each level, one by one. It was the early wins that gave us the encouragement and energy to spend the night conquering the harder levels.

If you've ever played a video game or even a puzzle app, you know what I'm talking about. Designers work hard to build games that are easy to learn but hard to master – carefully curating the difficulty of each level so that you feel challenged but never stuck.

One of the strongest tools in the toolbox for game designers is early wins. Almost always, early levels are quick and easy, building confidence and strategy for the challenge ahead. These early stages teach you the rules and tools of the game, while energizing and motivating you.

They also help you build momentum.

Momentum is critical for holding your gaming attention – and it works in real life too. If you establish habits that get you early wins each day, you'll start each day with the momentum needed to conquer the world.

Habits of self-discipline take time to establish. Time to bear fruit. Remember Willard's reliable pattern from chapter two? Early wins cement our intention. They take pressure off the willpower approach by feeding momentum.

Collecting early wins will keep you motivated while you learn the rules and tools of leadership. Early wins are concrete and tangible. They lay a foundation for the challenges ahead of you each day.

READY. SET. GO.

So, here's the easiest way to schedule an early win for yourself each day.

Make your bed.

When you wake up tomorrow, don't grab your phone and scroll. Don't hit snooze. Instead, get up and make your bed.

Making your bed is a concrete task. An easy win with tangible benefits. Within minutes of waking, you've already accomplished your first task of the day. And, as former Navy Admiral, William McCraven notes, making your bed will "give you a small sense of pride," and "encourage you to do another task, and another, and another."

Making your bed is an early win that can energize and motivate your day. And, like the first levels of any video game, making your bed builds momentum for the day – momentum that you'll need to face the difficult challenges ahead as you conquer the world.

I realize this may not feel game changing and there are other ways to grab an early win. That said, try making your bed everyday. If you already do, reframe it as a win and identify a next win you can build into your schedule - a cup of coffee in the quiet pre-dawn moments, putting on the exercise clothes you laid out the day before and getting the workout in, and on[1].

In fact, many of the habits in this book can count as an early win that builds momentum for your day. Whatever you pick, celebrate the early win and let it inspire you to conquer the day.

CHAPTER 10

HABIT 7
TRAIN YOUR BODY

> *It's been six months since I joined the gym, and still no progress! I'm going there in-person tomorrow to see what's going on.*

"SOMETHING'S GOT TO GIVE," I thought, adjusting my earbuds and logging into the umpteenth zoom call of the morning. Change is hard.

Work challenges were up, and my normal routine had been upended.

I could feel stress squeezing the muscles on my neck, shoulders, and upper back. I didn't have my office space, multiple screens, or a standing desk. Boundaries between family time and work were extra blurry working from home, and instead of walking around all day I was sitting in front of the screen for zoom meeting after zoom meeting.

"Download it," my wife quipped, as she floated past my dining table work station to pour another coffee between her own meetings.

It was an exercise app. She wanted me to join an exercise challenge – a pretty mild one requiring just 20 minutes of exercise, at least four times a week.

She said I needed it. I figured she was right, so I downloaded the app.

The next morning, I logged 20 minutes of exercise starting a streak of 103 days. As you might expect, I felt healthier. I got better sleep, lost the tension and headaches, and even dropped a few pounds.

I also got better at running. My pace dropped from eleven -minute miles to eight, and I increased how far I was running from 2 miles-a-day to 5 and 6 plus.

More important, I felt empowered. I saw significant improvement, and the benefits stretched far beyond health.

Running leaked into the rest of my life. My habit of daily exercise continues to foster self-discipline and grit while growing me as a leader in surprising ways. I've got a renewed sense of focus and clarity.

I believe your mind, body, and soul are deeply connected. When you take care of your body – establishing habits that train it – the benefits spill over, supporting your mind and soul as well.

READY. SET. GO.

So, to train your body, I challenge you to the same practice I established not long ago. Carve time – just 20 minutes each day – to exercise.

You can walk around the neighborhood, practice modified yoga, sit on a stationary bike, wheel yourself through the neighborhood, or lace up and go for a run like I did. Sometimes inclement weather or safety prevents neighborhood exercise. If so, stretch, lift, pull up YouTube videos - you have lots of options.

Make a commitment, and practice self-discipline, even when the weather doesn't cooperate. Your body will thank you. And, so will you mind and soul.

CHAPTER 11
HABIT 8
DESIGN A DAILY ROUTINE

> *No one laughs at my pre-workout routine joke.*
> *To be fair, it's a bit of a stretch.*

GOOD NEWS - You probably already follow a daily routine.

You already have set rhythms and habits that shape your daily life from morning to night. What do you do when you wake up? Do you scroll on your phone? Hit a snooze button? Bounce out of bed and into exercise clothes?

How do you answer emails? As they come? Twice a day?

Do you rearrange your work space daily? Weekly? Whenever it looks too piled to concentrate?

Unfortunately, the rhythms and habits you already have may not be the best for you. They may not serve you well. They may not help you stay grounded, connected, and productive.

So, I have some better news for you.

With a few intentional shifts, your daily routine can serve you. With some adjustments to the rhythms and habits you currently practice, you can experience greater freedom and balance while saving time and energy.

What many people fail to realize is this – a clear routine will actually free you.

Your daily routine has a huge impact on what you can accomplish. When you train yourself to follow a routine, doing the next hard thing gets easier – you don't have to fight preferences, you don't have to summon will power, or even make a choice. You simply submit your decision-making to the choices that "past you" already made about the best way to face today.

When you remove decision-making and the will power battle, the habits game changes.

READY. SET. GO.

What does this look like for you? Three simple steps. Let's unpack them one by one.

First, you'll need to identify the rhythms and habits you want to shape your day. Think about the bottle-necks and distractions you face. For instance, if you answer emails all day, make a change. Choose to answer email one or a few specific times each day.

Think about what you hope to accomplish, and how to make it easier. If you want to get morning exercise done, start laying out exercise clothes before you get in bed. Adding this to your daily routine will reduce the friction between waking and starting your run - cueing up the choice you want to make.

Once you've identified the right rhythms, sync them to your calendar. Consider your workflow, meetings, and varying energy throughout the day. Let those factors inform how you structure your daily calendar.

For instance, block actual time on your calendar for responding to email, and establish the habit of laying out exercise clothes right after you brush your teeth each night.

And, another tip – this one's free – habits stick faster when you stack them. It's easier to train yourself to lay out exercise clothes if you stack that practice onto brushing your teeth - an already fixed habit.

Finally, follow your routine. This is undoubtedly the hardest step.

If you've matched your new routine to values, you'll have the intrinsic motivation to get through a few days – maybe a few weeks.

If you've stacked your habits – made connections to the things you already do – your chance for long term success will skyrocket.

Will all this routine make life boring? I certainly hope not. The point here isn't to do the same thing all day everyday. The point is to establish practices that reflect alignment between your values and reality.

As you establish a daily routine, hold it loosely. Take things one day at a time, watch for points of friction you can remove, and be gracious with yourself. Having consistency in some areas - automating some behaviors with routine - will free headspace for other things. Establishing the right routine will take time, but stick with it. It'll be worth the effort.

CHAPTER 12
HABIT 9
SLEEP ON YOUR AGENDA

> *I was offered a job at a mattress factory. I asked them if I could sleep on it.*

THERE'S an African Proverb that says, "tomorrow belongs to the people who prepare for it today."

Everyone in our world is busy. You're busy. Your colleagues are busy. I'm busy. But busy isn't always productive, and unproductive busy leads to stress.

Successful leaders know how to work smarter. One of the keystone habits to a productive day is planning for it the night before.

I've got a few tips that will bring this habit to life, so you can implement it tonight, before you go to bed.

READY. SET. GO.

First, you'll need to hone your priorities. I've worked with so many clients who think they can conquer the world in a day.

They fill up their schedule, immediately fall behind. They often fall back to easier tasks that tick a box, pushing out the meaty work that really needs to get down.

> " The truth is, it's hard to tackle meaningful projects when you don't prioritize them.

You have to get realistic about your priorities, and you have to be realistic about the amount of time each priority will take. Weighing importance and time, pick the one or two pieces of work you most need to tackle.

Next, you'll need to get specific about what you're doing and when. Mark up your calendar with blocks of time devoted to those critical priorities. Turn off your notifications, let colleagues know you're busy, and focus on getting the work done.

Finally, add buffers and breaks to your day. For meetings, add 15-30 minutes so you have time to prepare and transition. This buffer will help remove the hurry, so you show up ready to engage, and remain present for the discussion.

For long stretches of work, add breaks. Studies show that not taking breaks leads to a lack of focus, decision fatigue, and if you spend your time in front of a screen, damaged eyes.

On the flip side, taking breaks has been shown to spark creativity while improving decision-making, focus, recall, and memory.

Your brain needs a pause so it can recharge (research in neurobiology confirms). I try to take a 10-15 minute break every 50 minutes. For most people, productivity takes a dive somewhere between 60 and 90 minutes.

Before that happens, take a walk, grab a coffee, take a nap, meditate, stretch, or eat a healthy snack. Detach from work, move away from your screen, and recharge.

Now that you've outlined priorities and carved specific time to achieve them, sleep on it. When you wake, you'll be ready to hit the ground running.

CHAPTER 13

HABIT 10
REFRAME GOALS

>   *I made it my goal to become a legal citizen of Finland and I'm not gonna quit... 'til I'm Finnish.*

EACH JANUARY, about 60% of Americans set New Year's resolutions and only about 8% achieve them. Goal setting is easy. Achieving those goals proves a bit more difficult.

Why is it that so many set resolutions and fail to achieve them?

Author Mark Manson offers a helpful reframe. What if happiness requires struggle? Do you want comfort? An amazing job? Deep relationships? Happiness? Yep, me too.

What are you willing to trade for those outcomes?

Or as Manson puts it:

>   What pain do you want in your life? What are you willing to struggle for?

Reframing goals in this way forces a commitment. How bad do you want it? This is especially powerful as you lead others. Reframing your goals will help you weigh your intention and underlying motivations. It'll force you to have a vision for you life that these goals might unlock. It will also prepare you to coach a team toward real goals that take significant effort and commitment.

Ready to reframe how you approach your goals?

I've got a few ideas to help you think differently about setting, reviewing, and achieving your goals.

READY. SET. GO.

First, you have to get really clear about the things you want to achieve and the order you need to achieve them in. You have to identify and prioritize your goals.

Distraction is the enemy of every goal, so whenever possible, narrow your list of goals. When you start in on your goals, start with one. Focus on that single most important goal.

When you complete it, add another. Tackling your list one goal at a time. Give the present goal your full attention.

Next, you need to identify the best system for achieving that goal. Author James Clear calls the goal a rudder, and he calls your system for achieving it the oars.

The rudder sets direction, but you won't make any progress if you don't paddle. For example, if your goal is to read 40 books this year, your system is the reading schedule. Your chance of accomplishing a goal go up exponentially when you discover the right system for achieving that goal.

Third, pay attention to your progress by reviewing your goals regularly. Tracking progress provides motivation and meaningful data. Our brains crave that kind of feedback and it builds momentum.

Finally, when you review your goals, ask yourself at least two hard questions:

First ask, Is this rudder still set in the right direction? Is this still the most important goal for you to paddle after?

In work and life, it's okay to reprioritize. Sometimes you need to push through your priorities in their current order despite the difficulties. Keep that rudder locked in. Other times, things change, and shifting from one priority to another may be the right decision. When that happens, adjust the rudder.

Second ask, What friction is keeping you from moving faster? You might have process issues, people challenges, funding hurdles, and on. Once you've identified relevant points of friction, find ways to remove them. What changes can you make that will help you achieve your goals faster?

Thinking differently about goals will help you set and chase them more effectively. With focus and the right system, you'll be well on your way to maintaining resolutions, and achieving more at work and at home.

CHAPTER 14

HABIT 11

PRACTICE DEEP WORK

> *I used to work at an orange juice factory. I just couldn't concentrate, so they put the squeeze on me.*

OUR WORLD IS full of distractions. We have email, social media, swaths of productivity apps, phones more powerful than the computers that put a man on the moon. Our distractions tug on our attention constantly. As a result, our ability to concentrate is splintered.

While it's a popular myth that humans have a shorter attention span (8 seconds) than goldfish (9 seconds), research *does* suggest that our attention spans are decreasing.[1] Further, this digital age has reduced our ability to give sustained and selective attention. Instead, we increasingly rely on divided attention which decreases performance.

The result? Our ability to concentrate – to focus and make meaningful progress on what design theorist and professor Horst Rittel dubbed "wicked problems" – is becoming increasingly rare and increasingly valuable.

Successful leaders develop habits that allow for deep work to get done. Author Cal Newport lays out the importance of pushing your cognitive capabilities to their limit in a distraction free environment. Carving distraction free time to tackle wicked problems.

Many spend their work days perpetually distracted - constantly switching their attention between activities or multi-tasking. As a result, the big tasks and wicked problems never get appropriate attention.

When you practice deep work, you learn to master hard things and produce at an *elite* level. But, this requires high levels of concentration and focus.[2]

> (Deep Work is any) professional activity performed in a state of distraction-free concentration that push(es) your cognitive capabilities to their limit. These efforts create new value, improve your skill, and are hard to replicate.
>
> CAL NEWPORT

Deep work can look like focused research, data analysis, developing strategy, or drafting content. If you're not already practicing deep work – focused, distraction-free, concentration for chunks of time – I've got some tips to help you start practicing this critical habit.

READY. SET. GO.

First, start scheduling time for deep work. Identify extended blocks of time when you can shift your environment, eliminate distractions, and tackle wicked problems. At first, aim for just an hour each day – or two 25 minute blocks if you're a fan of the Pomodoro Method. Try to schedule deep work in the morning when you are freshest. Deep work is taxing. It takes real effort and energy. That first hour will take a toll. Over time, you'll be able to expand that hour to 4 or more hours of deep work in a day.

When you finish deep work, take a real break. Work hard, and then play. One way to make your breaks a habit is by establishing a *transition ritual*. When your deep work ends, what habit will you *stack* on the end – a walk? A nap? Create a ritual that rewards the work and gives your brain well-earned downtime to recharge.

Finally, pay attention to your internet use. If you really want to practice deep work, start scheduling your internet connectivity. Only connect when you need to be connected - and schedule those times. This practice will help you dial down the noise by eliminating the incessant notifications that plague you.

This is especially important as your work day ends. Internet connectivity trains you to practice splintered attention. This hinders your deep work capacity and the related cognitive success. As much as possible, cut the proverbial cord - or the real ethernet cable. Read a book. Be present with people.

As a leader, your habit of deep work will equip you to tackle wicked problems and lead others with insight. It's a rare skill, and your company will value your ability to produce at an elite level.

PART FOUR
HABITS FOR THE
RELATIONAL SELF

If you want to go fast, go alone.
If you want to go far, go together.

AFRICAN PROVERB

CHAPTER 15

HABIT 12
CULTIVATE GRATITUDE

> *How do generals show gratitude to their troops?*
> *They give tanks.*

A FEW YEARS AGO, I started a gratitude journal with a goal – list ten thousand things I'm thankful for. At first, I was pretty consistent – listing three things a day. After a few months I set the journal down and didn't pick it back up. A few months passed, and I started again – a pattern that has continued to today.

As I reflect on my on-again-off-again adoption of the gratitude journal, I can say with confidence that I am more grounded, more fun to be around, and more productive when keeping the journal.

Intentionally practicing gratitude has been very good for me. It's a habit I find so valuable, I've tried to instill the habit in my kids.

Flexing your gratitude muscle will impact your attitude. Research ties gratitude to improved productivity, stronger relationships, enhanced well-being, resilience, and self-advocacy.

And, gratitude doesn't just strengthen your thinking and working – it also impacts your physical health. Studies report better sleep, quicker heart attack recovery, decreased risk of heart failure, reduced stress, fewer reported aches and pains, and on. The literature around gratitude is, well, something to be thankful for.

So, how do you begin a habit of gratitude? I've got two practices that have worked for me. Take your pick.

READY. SET. GO.

First, you could start a gratitude journal. Multiple studies report that those who keep a gratitude journal for two to ten weeks report fewer headaches, less stomach issues, clearer skin, and reduced congestion.

When you do, be sure to fill it in with "long tail" gratitudes[1]. If you're familiar with keyword searching, you've heard of short-tail and long tail keywords. Apply that notion to your gratitude – go beyond listing short-tail thanks like "good friends," or "time with family."

Get specific. Use long-tail gratitudes like, "warm evenings watching the sun set beyond Campus Point as my kids wrap up an afternoon of surfing."

Don't forget to schedule time for gratitude.

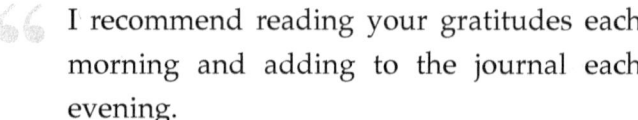 I recommend reading your gratitudes each morning and adding to the journal each evening.

The second habit is serving others. You're probably thinking, "Yeah, service makes sense once I'm grateful. I mean, once we realize all that we have, we give to others out of that abundance."

In reality, it's a chicken-egg thing. Sure, we can serve out of the abundance of our gratitude.

> Moreover, we can jumpstart gratitude by serving.

Serving others is a quick and active way to stop thinking about yourself. When you shift your perspective to serving others, you realize the capacity you have to give. It confirms how much you have to be grateful for.

At my house this looks like getting my laundry put away quickly, and doing the dishes when it's not my turn. It also looks like time in my community distributing canned goods or supporting our local rescue mission. What does it look like for you?

Whichever habit you choose to foster, do it intentionally. Take the practical steps needed to schedule, commit, and follow through on the practice. When you do, it'll give you one more reason to be grateful.

FOR MORE READING *on gratitude research, here's a sampling to get you started:*

Achor, S. (2010). *The happiness advantage: How a positive brain fuels success in work and life.* Currency.

Emmons, R. A., & Mishra, A. (2011). Why gratitude enhances well-being: What we know, what we need to know. In K. M. Sheldon, T. B. Kashdan, & M. F. Steger (Eds.), *Designing positive psychology: Taking stock and moving forward* (pp. 248–262). Oxford University Press.

Smith, J. A., Newman, K., Marsh, J., & Keltner, D. (2020). *The gratitude project: how the science of thankfulness can rewire our brains for resilience, optimism, and the greater good.* Oakland, CA: New Harbinger Publications, Inc.

Starkey, A. R., Mohr, C. D., Cadiz, D. M., & Sinclair, R. R. (2019). Gratitude reception and physical health: Examining the mediating role of satisfaction with patient care in a sample of acute care nurses. *The Journal of Positive Psychology, 14*(6), 779-788.

Wood, A. M., Joseph, S., Lloyd, J., & Atkins, S. (2009). Gratitude influences sleep through the mechanism of pre-sleep cognitions. *Journal of psychosomatic research, 66*(1), 43-48.

CHAPTER 16

HABIT 13
STAY CURIOUS

> *Which letter of the alphabet is the most curious?*
> *Y.*

SUCCESSFUL LEADERS GET REALLY good at being curious. You must. You don't want to be the smartest person in the room.

You *need* smarter people giving you real feedback – good answers and hard questions. You have to let others - and their expertise - inform your thinking and decision-making[1].

> "If I had an hour to solve a problem, I'd spend fifty-five minutes thinking about the problem."
>
> ALBERT EINSTEIN

This takes patience.

Genuine curiosity requires vulnerability. You can't

hold tightly to an answer when you get curious. When you start asking honest questions, you have to let go of controlling the outcome. Being curious requires you to ask with an open mind and an open hand.

In *Dare to Lead*, Brene Brown writes,

> "Curiosity says: no worries. I love a wild ride. I'm up for wherever this goes. And, I'm in for however long it takes to get to the heart of the problem. I don't know the answers or have to say the right thing, I just have to keep listening and keep questioning."

She's absolutely right. A habit of curiosity will open doors of opportunity. You will strengthen relationships with your peers and grow trust across your teams.

So, how can you cultivate genuine curiosity? I have a few tips to get you started.

READY. SET. GO.

First, if you're someone who likes to be right, start loosening your grip. Wanting to be right will stifle curiosity. Instead of an open mind, wanting to be right leads to walls and defense.

This starts before you show up. Having the right expectations for a meeting or engagement will allow you to practice curiosity. Reframe those expectations before you show up – the goal is to learn and understand, not to win.

Next, when you show up, be present. In our distracted world, we trade deep investment for shallow accomplishment of many tasks. Don't fall into this trap – especially when it comes to relationships. I believe people want to be known and loved. This simply can't happen when we allow distractions to pull our attention away.

Being curious means being attentive – actually listening to the answers. Stop thinking of rebuttals, and concentrate on listening. Listen to the answer, the tone, the non-verbals. What can you learn?

Finally, practice asking lots of open and clarifying questions. Say things like, "Tell me more about...", "Help me understand...", or the 3-word AWE question, "and what else..." from Michael Stanier's *The Coaching Habit*.

Dig in. Focus on understanding. Listen attentively to the answers.

Follow this playbook and your grip on being right will naturally loosen. Remember, you never want to be the smartest person in the room. Lean on the collective wisdom, and build relationships along the way.

CHAPTER 17
HABIT 14

ASSUME POSITIVE INTENT

> *Most people assume pirates join the navy, but it turns out they prefer the arrrrrrrrmy.*

I DO A REALLY great job of assuming that my own intentions are pure. When they aren't, I'm able to construct robust justifications for my actions.

Not surprisingly, I have a harder time doing this for others.

Brene Brown talks about this storytelling skill in Dare to Lead – people take bits of disconnected information and string them together in a way that best fits their perspective.

Unfortunately, when you construct stories about what has happened and why others have behaved a particular way, you tend to lean on unreliable and negative influences - like biases, anxieties, and fears.

This combination rarely colors others in the best possible light.

Successful leaders cultivate a habit that puts others

in the best possible light. They practice assuming positive intent.

What would happen if you assumed your work colleagues were doing their best? What if you assumed their intent was positive – even when it didn't feel true or authentic?

I believe this is one of the keys to effective leadership at all levels. So, how do you practice assuming positive intent? I've got a few ideas to get you started.

READY. SET. GO.

First, you'll have to retrain your storytelling brain, by interrogating it. Pay attention to when you start building a story. Before it gets fully developed, start asking yourself questions that broaden or challenge your storytelling brain. For instance,

- What information is missing?
- What assumptions are you making?
- How would the subject of your story tell things?

Asking questions like these help you *retrain* your storytelling brain to build more empathic stories that assume positive intent.

Now, this doesn't mean you let problems slide. As a philosophy graduate student, I spent a lot of time critiquing arguments – including my own. I suspect you don't have to be a philosophy student to get good at this. We do it all the time in work settings.

Approach others charitably - imagining the best possible version of their position. To do this, you'll need to layer empathy into storytelling process. You'll have to practice seeing thought processes from the other perspectives.

TRY A PRACTICE SCENARIO:

Think about a colleague who frustrated you recently. Let your mind retell that story. Now, practice assuming positive intent by interrogating your story.

Flex your empathy muscles. Re-imagine the interaction from their perspective. Imagine your colleague did their best work with good intentions. How many different ways can you play the scenario out?

Finally, write down a few honest, non-judgmental, and forward-thinking questions you could ask that colleague, to further understand what happened and open the door for feedback. This charitable approach invites you to presume good intentions and guides you to the kinds of questions that might clarify what really happened in the frustrating situation.

Keep in mind that there will be times you assume positive intent and it becomes clear that the person frustrating you *did not* act with positive intent.

It happens. Sometimes people really are out to get you.

But catch this – even then, assuming positive intent will help you move forward in a positive way.

Assuming positive intent is a strategy that works even when it shouldn't.

Finally, reflect on your practice. What changed for you? Were you able to see things from a different perspective? How does the new perspective inform your relationship?

As a practice, assuming positive intent will change your relationships and your outlook. It's amazing how quickly you'll begin to see the flaws in your own intentions, and the good in those around you. It's a practice that inspires realistic optimism - I hope it also brings you joy.

CHAPTER 18
HABIT 15
PRACTICE INSPIRING

> *For motivation, my friend buys a new rug every day. His motto is 'carpet diem.'*

INSPIRATION HAS a lot to do with connection – with *belonging*.

I still have this bubble memory of 16-year old me sitting on a granite boulder in the High Sierras, facing the largest of the Graveyard Lakes. Rocky ridges rose behind the still water. It was a crisp morning, and as the sun rose, steam lifted from the lake.

I remember that particular morning because something strange happened inside me as I sipped my coffee – something almost spiritual. Maybe you've had a similar experience in a wild space. I had this unique moment of belonging – a sense the world was much bigger than I had previously known, and I had a place in it.

I could feel my spirit lift. I felt inspired, motivated to live well.

Do you remember the last time you felt inspired? Maybe it was a moment in nature, a book you read, a coach's speech, a note from a friend or mentor.

Inspiration doesn't have to happen on a silent ridgeline as the sun rises. The secret to inspiring and motivating your people? It's really about *belonging* – deep, authentic connection. Inspiration calls you out of your mundane routine, by reframing your daily life in a bigger, more meaningful context.

Successful leaders have developed this ability to inspire – to reframe work in a way that calls out the value and meaning you provide to something bigger. Leaders practice inspiring and motivating their people because they know that, like any habit, inspiration is a something you can you get better at over time.

I've got three tips to break down what it takes to inspire and motivate your people.

READY. SET. GO.

First, be yourself. Authenticity builds trust. Whenever possible, stop performing.

In your meetings – formal and informal – live your values, share your passions, and stay grounded in your why. Your people will connect with these values and passions. It's likely a big part of why they work for you.

It's been said that people don't leave companies, they leave their bosses. The inverse is also true. An inspiring boss can fill a tireless or thankless job with meaning and purpose.

Second, make explicit connections between the work

and why it matters. When you share your appreciation for an employee's hard work, explain how that specific work links to broader impacts. Like the NASA janitor who told JFK he was helping put a man on the moon, you want your people to embrace their work as vocation – as a calling to the shared passions and values of your workplace.

Finally, fight for frequency and proximity with your people. Cementing an inspired sense of *belonging* takes relationship – and relationship takes time.

The coach's halftime speech inspires the team - not because it has all the right words, but because the coach is speaking it. Remember, that's the same coach who showed up every day, got dirty alongside the team, and built deep relationships.

Building deep relationships takes frequency and proximity. You have to prioritize time with your people. Over time, your credibility to inspire can skyrocket. With the amount of noise people face today, frequency and proximity are your best inroad to deeper connection.

It's true. Inspiration happens in nature and through TED talks, but don't overlook the daily opportunity you have to inspire your people by reminding them of the impact of their work – especially as it connects to your shared values and passions.

CHAPTER 19
HABIT 16
GROW CONNECTIONS

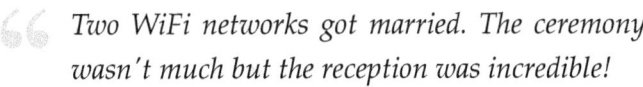 *Two WiFi networks got married. The ceremony wasn't much but the reception was incredible!*

IN OUR FIVE years as Denver-ites, I fell in love with aspen trees – their bark, the sound of wind rustling their leaves. Then, I learned how unique they are. They're typically only found above 5k feet, and they grow as a colony – sharing the same root system, sending new shoots up to grow an expansive network of trees.

Networking – expanding your relationships – is not unlike a growing aspen.

Successful leaders recognize the importance of building far reaching connections linked by strong roots. Like the aspen, a healthy network will provide you with *rootedness* and *support*.

So, what does it take to get over the fear of making new friendships? What will it take for you to lean in and build invaluable relationships?

I've got a few tips to help you develop a habit of relationship building that will expand your network and provide you with invaluable rootedness and support.

READY. SET. GO.

First, create some buckets to help you think about current and potential connections. Make a list of the people you spend time with – directs, peers, colleagues, friends. Then use the buckets to make sense of how they might root and support you in your career.

For instance, some relationships will ground your *operational thinking* – your understanding of your current work and ability to get things done in your current organization.

Others will be more personal – those who support your *leadership development*.

Still others will support you *strategically* – linking you to stakeholders or new opportunities.

As you fill each bucket with current contacts, pay attention to the gaps. Where do you need to grow wider roots? Where do you need more support?

Second, work to fill the gaps you identified. Be intentional about your relationship building. As a newcomer to the zoo profession, I pursued an executive leadership development program that would shore up my zoo chops while introducing me to folks that knew a lot more about the profession than I did.

In that year, I built dozens of strong relationships with peers and mentors across the profession. Some as a direct result of the program, and others because I got intentional about visiting other zoos and aquariums, and connecting with their leaders. My current thinking and leading is rooted and supported by those relationships – operationally, personally, and strategically.

Third, when reaching out to new contacts, express genuine interest. Be a learner. Pursue relationships with interesting people and learn from them. Seek out colleagues doing similar work in other industries – what can you learn from their approach? Seek out C-suite peers who oversee vastly different functions or businesses – what can you draw from their experience? Remember, you never want to be the smartest person in the proverbial room.

Finally, provide value. Be, as Tommy Spaulding says, a net-giver instead of a networker. Net giving is about others – how can you support, elevate, and honor others as you build relationship with them. Reciprocity is a real thing. When we approach relationships ready to give, we can build them authentically. And, asking for help or advice gives someone a chance to impact your life. Sometimes that's value enough.

What if you feel like you have no value to offer?

I've heard this concern from clients and students alike. The short answer is this - you *can* provide value. Don't believe the lie that you have nothing to offer. You can give encouragement, resources, a testimonial, and on.

Net-giving is not transactional gamesmanship. This isn't an opportunity to manipulate others so that you generate feelings of reciprocity. Be your (professional) self.

> Net-givers approach relationship building from an authentic place of service.

Make habits of these four steps – schedule them into your calendar. It's okay to be strategic – to schedule time with connections to ask questions or provide value – especially when you approach relationships authentically.

PART FIVE
HABITS FOR THE
DISCERNING SELF

Discernment is the son of good judgement and the father of self-control.

CRISS JAMI

CHAPTER 20

HABIT 17
FIND A GUIDE

Are you ready to take these 'Dad Jokes' to the next level? Follow me upstairs.

WHILE RUNNING a nonprofit I founded to develop leaders through challenge, I got to take a group of students to the Bahamas for a sailing adventure. The first day aboard our 64' vessel, one student was nominated to captain the trip. This student would be responsible for leading the crew as we sailed between islands.

The catch? None of our students knew how to sail. The owner of the boat – the real captain – would serve as a guide.

His mentorship, as you can imagine, provided an invaluable service to our students. Captain Steve knew the ocean floor, the currents, and the local wind patterns. He also knew his boat intimately – where every rope and pulley rested. And, he knew how to sail - when to unfurl what sail when, how to use the wind with the vessel.

Without Steve, our student captain couldn't have led the team out of Nassau harbor. With Steve, the crew navigated shallow shoals and crossed a tight channel in shifting tides.

You need a captain Steve. Successful leaders recognize their need for guidance. They clear space in their schedules to receive mentorship and coaching.

As a leader yourself, you probably already play the role of Captain Steve for others.

- Who comes to you for advice?
- Who relies on you as a sounding board?
- Who regularly taps into your experience in exchange for a coffee or pint?

These are the people who already see *you* as a guide, coach, or mentor.

What about you? Who is your sounding board? You need to carve intentional time with people you admire – not just to learn, but to invite feedback and coaching.

I've had the opportunity to coach lots of executives and early stage entrepreneurs over the last few years – acting as their sounding board, encouraging growth, and providing accountability. And, I recognize the value enough to seek out my own guides and mentors.

Finding the right guides and mentors doesn't have to be difficult. I've got a few suggestions to point you in the right direction.

READY. SET. GO.

First, think about how you want to grow. Captain Steve served as a very specific kind of guide. While he happens to be good at a lot of things, our students leaned on his guidance for how to sail.

What skills are you hoping to shore up? What facets of personal growth are holding you back professionally? Getting clear about your goals and timeline will help you identify the right kind of coach.

Once you're clear about your goals, seek out a guide with those specific skills. Consider their skill set, alongside their values and personality. Ask yourself, will this relationship be a good fit? Will I accept challenge and feedback from this person? In my experience, shared values go a long way in coaching relationships. Do some research, and identify potential guides that have the expertise, values, and personality needed to help you move forward.

Next, you'll need to start a conversation. Depending on your selection, this might be anything from a cold email to a casual coffee. Both can work – and everything in between.

Try to feel out your potential mentor. For some, naming your relationship mentoring will introduce all kinds of baggage and expectation. For others, knowing exactly what you need up front will accelerate the process.

When I meet with clients in a formal coaching setting, we get clear about goals and metrics in our first 90 minutes. That allows us to hit the ground running.

Finally, dig in. Take the lead by preparing an agenda for meetings. Share honestly, listen well, ask for feedback, and let the relationship grow.

While it can be intimidating to open up to a guide, coach, or mentor, it's essential to your growth as a leader. Remember, you never want to be the smartest person in the room. With a guide, you never have to be.

CHAPTER 21
HABIT 18
PRACTICE STORYTELLING

> *My dog can spin a great story. Unfortunately, he only has one tail.*

I HAD a chance to work at an upstart secondary school in Denver that grew from 150 students in year two, to over 900 when I left in year six. Each year the faculty doubled.

Like any rapidly growing start-up, school leaders worked hard to over-communicate cultural norms and establish rituals that anchored faculty to our school's unique approach.

Each fall, before the semester, the entire faculty and staff team would attend a three-day offsite retreat. We played together, broke bread together, and planned together.

One staple of each retreat came when the Head shared the school's origin story. It didn't matter how many times you had heard it before. The story was compelling. It placed the current school year into a bigger context. It connected individual roles to a vision that was less about lesson planning or student activities and more about raising up future leaders.

It took a vision that a handful of people held some years before, connected it to a vision our faculty and staff embraced, and suggested hope in our ability to achieve it.

Have you heard a vision cast like that before?

If you have, I'd wager that at least these four things happened:

1. You felt deep connection to something important and bigger than yourself.
2. You felt that connection emotionally.
3. The connection linked to your passion or values.
4. And, you came away from that moment more hopeful.

Successful leaders learn to cast vision through stories that connect their people to broader goals. Practicing this kind of intentional storytelling – what I call vision reframing – will strengthen your organization's clarity and focus around what matters most.

So, how do you make a habit of telling these kinds of stories? I've got a few tips to get you started.

READY. SET. GO.

First, reflect on the stories you have to share. We all have experiences to share. Start making a list of the stories you like to tell. If you don't have many, start a new piece of paper with a list of years on the left – going backwards from the current year.

Then, jot down a few interesting things that took place in each year. As you do, your mind will flood with memories – key in on the memories that linked to your values and passions. Those are stories you'll want to tell.

Next, tell the story. Whether you type it, dictate it to a recorder, or tell it to a friend, make the memory concrete in story form by telling it.

Now, practice. Don't wait for the annual retreat or a quarterly all hands to tell your stories. Instead, look for connections in the mundane of work that you can reframe around your bigger vision. Practice relaying that vision to your team through story.

Don't forget to make strong connections. Think about how the story links to organizational goals and values. Use stories to call out how specific people are doing important things today that will lead the organization to the goals of tomorrow.

Finally, seek feedback. Becoming a good storyteller takes practice. Well told stories move us. Think critically about your storytelling:

- Is the theme clear?
- Have you borrowed from the hero's journey?

- How's your timing?
- When will you pause for emphasis?
- When might you anticipate laughter?

Remember, story-telling is a craft. Be patient with yourself and practice often. Before you know it, vision reframing will come naturally, and your people will feel more connected and focused because of it.

CHAPTER 22

HABIT 19
PRACTICE FILTERING DECISIONS

> *Counselor: Your partner allows you to make independent decisions?*
> *Me: *looks at wife**
> *Wife: *nods**
> *Me: Yes, of course.*

SO, what does it take to practice good decision-making? I recommend three filters that will help you make quicker, clearer, and more effective decisions.

Before looking at the filters, keep a couple of things in mind:

1. When it comes to decision making, you always have more than two options.
2. Not all decisions have to be made. Ask yourself if the decision you are considering is urgent. Can you sleep on it? Put it off all together? If so, do.

3. Try to zoom out when making difficult
   decisions – think in years, not days.

That said, here are three filters you apply – like a ritual – to ease the weight of tough decisions.

READY. SET. GO.

First, filter each decision through your imagination. Force yourself to create a variety of alternative choices. Feel free to get silly. Explore what you could do, the potential outcomes, and their impact.

Then, assign rough probabilities to each outcome. This exercise will force you to think more holistically about the context for the decision, and should surface even more live options.

Second, you need to filter any possible decision through your values. Having clearly understood values is critical. Print out your values and display them somewhere prevalent. Review them regularly.

Your values filter will help you assess values-alignment in any possible decision. You'll want to think long and hard about decisions that create friction with your values. Whatever the perceived gain, it's probably not worth it.

Third, use your mission and vision as a filter for potential decisions – again, assessing for alignment. Consider how live options will impact your company aspirations and how you plan to get there? Narrow your options to those that best support your goals and trajectory.

As you practice using these filters, you'll find yourself becoming more decisive – and that's a good thing.[1]

CHAPTER 23
HABIT 20
ALWAYS BE READING

> *I spent all day reading - I suppose it was bound to happen. When it comes to books I have no shelf control.*

I'M a huge fan of books. Sir Isaac Newton stood on shoulders, I stand on stacks and stacks of books.

I like podcasts and online articles too, but for me, nothing beats sitting down with a real, physical book, a pen or pencil, and a steaming cup of coffee. I like to feel the paper, and turn the page. I like to underline and star the text. I even track arguments and ask questions in the margin.

I've tried to switch to digital – which certainly has some advantages – but in the end, I learn best with a physical book. I can often picture where on a page I read something – even before I remember the page or the book I read it in.

Whether you like blogs, magazines, or books, one of the secrets of leadership success is to keep reading.

Successful leaders never stop learning. A high level of input – reading across topics and genres, will keep your mind turning with new ideas and connections that lead to clarity, focus, and innovation.

So, how do you pick up a habit of reading? I've got two suggestions to help you get started.

READY. SET. GO.

First, like any habit, you'll need to carve time. As a leader, you'll need to develop an understanding of broader contexts.

If you're an executive, you'll need to identify and articulate connections across functions and industries. Reading widely will strengthen your ability to make those connections. As you read, consider how the reading aligns with or informs your work environment.

Second, don't limit yourself to the business or personal growth shelves.

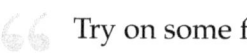 Try on some fiction.

Dive into a Tolstoy, Cathers, or Salinger every now and again. You may be surprised how relevant their stories are to your work context – the way they capture the human spirit in characters who parallel our present contexts.

Consider the relevance of verse written by Langston Hughes a hundred years ago, or Thoreau a hundred years before that. Volumes of wisdom rest at our finger tips, and while Austen and Hemingway can't teach you to write code, they can teach you a lot about people.

Try on some history or politics. Dig into philosophy if you have the patience – or want to overcome insomnia. Whatever you choose to read, keep at it with an eye for *synthesis*.

> How might this drama, or story, or poem, or concept - how might this wisdom - inform your thinking and working as you lead others?

As Dr. Seuss penned, "The more that you read, the more things you will know. The more that you learn, the more places you'll go."

Best of all, this habit is easy to start. Look around your house or office today and start with whatever strikes your interests first. There's no need to start with what seems most impressive or important - who knows what you'll know tomorrow.

FINAL THOUGHTS

> *One bird can't finish an entire bowl of Fruit Loops...but Toucan.*

Congrats, you did it!

You made it to the end - which as you know, is just the beginning. Hopefully you've got a clear vision and lots of tools to help you get there.

Now you face the hard work of commitment. Are you going to put this book down and forget about it? Or, are you ready to put these tools to work for you.

If you need support, please reach out. Habits are powerful things - and your life will be changed with each practice.

A FEW GOOD BOOKS

If you're interested in learning more about habits as you grow your leadership, there are some great books out there. You can check out *The Power of Habit*, by Charles

Duhigg, *Atomic Habits*, by James Clear, but I think my favorite is *Good Habits, Bad Habits*, by Wendy Wood.

I also encourage you to pick up Brene Brown's *Dare to Lead*. While it isn't directly about habits, it offers some great tips for developing healthy office relationships.

ADDITIONAL RESOURCES

Finally, forming new habits can be tough - especially on your own, armed with just a book (even a really good one with a tree on the cover). Reading is only step one.

We've developed additional resources to support you on your "grounded & growing" leadership journey:

- Get Connected
- Download our *"Ready. Set. Go. Worksheets"*
- Download bonus *"Grounding Exercises"*
- Track Your Growth

All these resources are available at:

https://habitsforleadersbooklaunch.carrd.co

I look forward to seeing you there.

MENTIONED RESOURCES

Aristotle, & Beresford, A. (2020). *The Nicomachean ethics.*
Brown, B. (2018). *Dare to Lead: Brave Work. Tough Conversations. Whole Hearts.* Random House.

Eblin, S. (2018). *The next level: What insiders know about executive success.*

Clear, J. (2018). *Atomic habits: Tiny changes, remarkable results : an easy & proven way to build good habits & break bad ones.*

Manson, Mark. https://markmanson.net

Newport, C. A. L. (2018). *Deep Work: Rules for focused success in a distracted world.* Grad Central Pub.

Spaulding, T. (2012). *It's Not Just Who You Know: Transform Your Life (And Your Organization) by Turning Colleagues and Contacts into Lasting, Genuine Relationships.* Random House Inc.

Stanier, M. B. (2016). *The coaching habit: Say less, ask more & change the way you lead forever.* Box of Crayons Press.

Sinek, Simon (2009). "How great leaders inspire action." TEDxPuget Sound.

Willard, D. (2021). *Renovation of the heart: Putting on the character of Christ.*

Wood, W. (2021). *Good habits, bad habits: The science of making positive changes stick.*

NOTES

3. VISION & INTENTION

1. Need more structure? You're not alone. I've got two exercises to help you get "visiony" about your own life. You can find them both at the end of Chapter 4 - in the section titled *Ready. Set. Go.*

5. HABIT 2

1. The enneagram is a personality framework that highlights both the virtues and vices that drive variously wired people. I have found it to be a helpful framework for thinking about the vices most likely to entrap me, and the coping strategies I adopted that once helped me navigate life but may not serve me any longer. While there are free assessments online, I would encourage those interested to start by reading through the nine types and attending to the darker side of each. Experience suggests that you'll be ready to self-identify with a number when you cringe at the more difficult aspects of a particular description because you recognize those tendencies in yourself. A final caveat, the enneagram is a tool, not a label.

6. HABIT 3

1. You can read about the study here: https://nautil.us/this-is-your-brain-on-silence-2251/
2. And another study here - https://www.inc.com/betsy-mikel/your-brain-benefits-most-when-you-listen-to-absolutely-nothing-science-says.html

8. HABIT 5

1. Several early readers noted the gendered nature of this story - and they are right. I want acknowledge the warrior narrative is tired and baggage-laden. In response, I have replaced "knight" with "hero/heroine" with the hope that this removes some distraction from the analogy.

9. HABIT 6

1. Thanks to early reader Gary Reynolds who adds that getting an early win at work can reframe the day. He suggests finding an early win to celebrate right after lunch as well. I concur.

14. HABIT 11

1. Thanks to Dr. Estelle Sandhaus for challenging the human:goldfish attention span myth. For a brief overview and links to additional research, check out this article: https://turtl.co/blog/the-attention-span-myth/
2. Read more about deep work here - https://blog.doist.com/deep-work/#Choose_Your_Deep_Work_Strategy

15. HABIT 12

1. Thanks to early reader DJ Lang who connects this notion of long-tail gratitude to brain research presented by the Huberman Lab podcast (11.22.21)

16. HABIT 13

1. Thanks to early reader Katie Manion who noted that opening this book up to be read and edited by a large team of readers and asking, "what do you think?" is an example of staying curious. It required vulnerability, and the result is a much stronger final product because more voices were included.

22. HABIT 19

1. Thanks to early reader Michelle Caprio who drew strong parallels between this chapter and the work being done at the Brain Health Team in Dallas. For more support and a self-paced course, check out https://centerforbrainhealth.org/training.

ACKNOWLEDGMENTS

> *Knock knock.*
> *Who's there?*
> *Tank.*
> *Tank who?*
> *No, thank you.*

There are many people to thank for the outworking of this book. Those who taught me about habits, those who helped me lose a few, and those who helped me start some too.

I'm grateful to the 75,000 and counting who have viewed and continue to view early versions of this content as a digital course. I'm grateful to the Made-Craft team for suggesting I develop the content in the first place. I'm grateful for a partner and kids who tolerate my many projects.

I'm grateful to all the friends who dove in with me on this project, reading various versions and providing incredible feedback. This project represents my learning at so many levels - in life, in school, and from you in this editing process - and processing/integrating your feedback has been a great joy. You know who you are. Please know that I am deeply grateful.

During the editing process a friend shared what I receive as a high compliment:

> "I think it is a good, simple primer. I've enjoyed it. It has been fun reading the way you've crystalized items that I know you've been thinking about for years. Also, I enjoyed seeing how you weave your faith through it without it being overtly Christian. I think it is accessible to a range of readers in a great way. Really well done."

I want to believe him. I hope it has been a practical tool that draws on ancient wisdom to help us navigate our convoluted and over-committed realities. I hope I have shared a bit of who I am with you.

I mention this because ultimately, I am grateful for you - the reader. I am grateful that you decided to take this journey with me, and I hope the investment has been worthy of your time.

ABOUT THE AUTHOR

Aaron is an entrepreneur and C-suite executive with more than a dozen years advising & coaching leaders to get clear, strategic, and focused so they can scale their businesses and grow their impact.

His academic journey in character formation (MA, Philosophy '08), experiential learning (PhD, Education '17), and business (Executive MBA '22) blends nicely with his practical business experience across sectors: as a brick-and-mortar entrepreneur, digital entrepreneur, NPO Founder, coach, consultant, & Zoo COO.

Beyond that, Aaron enjoys speaking, teaching Social Entrepreneurship for Westmont College, serving as affiliate faculty at Penn State's Kurt Hahn Consortium for Values & Experiential Learning, and serving through board and committee work.

Aaron has published a variety of content including a series of kids books about what it means to be a hero, video courses on culture and habits, as well as peer-reviewed journal articles and book chapters at the intersection of personal/social development and experiential learning.

He and his brilliant wife Janay have three children. As often as possible, you'll find them enjoying life together - hiking, biking, paddling, skating, or surfing - in Santa Barbara.

Want to keep the conversation going?

Connect with Aaron at armarshall.com or LinkedIn.

in linkedin.com/in/aaron-r-marshall

The Book of Self:

"In the Now of Knowing and Going"

INicole Royce

www.TrueVinePublishing.org

The Book of Self
By INicole Royce

Published by True Vine Publishing Co.
P.O. Box 22448
Nashville, TN 37202
www.TrueVinePublishing.org

ISBN: 978-0-57825753-2

Printed in the United States—First Printing